Impressions of
Holland Park

Gli
Ori
london

Impressions of
Holland Park

Photography by Gry Iverslien
Introduction by Michael Jacobs

To Sylvia Tobert Katz
and in memory of Christopher Wood,
the late chairman of
The Friends of Holland Park

Published by **Gli Ori** london

Photography copyright © Gry Iverslien 2002
Text copyright © Michael Jacobs 2002

Scanning: Screenservice, Comeana, Italy
Printing: Conti Tipocolor, Calenzano, Italy

ISBN 88-7336-042-4

Front cover: close-up of an Indian Blue Peacock
Title page: the old gates at the south entrance of Holland Park

Earth would be less fair without trees to grace her valleys, Hide her scars cast cool shade, In gardens here.

Impressions of Holland Park

Michael Jacobs

Half a century ago, when the grounds of Holland House were offered as a public park, the gardens had been reduced to what one artist visitor described as a 'gorgeous romantic ruin'. Though nothing today attests to this former neglected state, the park has come down to us as a series of eloquent and often enticingly enigmatic fragments. The early impressions on wandering around the park are likely to be confusing, as you proceed from what appears to be the bosky heart of the countryside to gardens laid out in a pseudo-Renaissance manner, encountering in the process a miscellany of sculptural and architectural relics that seem like the uncohesive figments from a dream.

The one overriding emotion on first entering Holland Park is the surprise of finding such a place at all in the middle of a bustling city. A private property for over three and a half centuries, with a Jacobean mansion at its heart, this is virtually the only grand ancestral estate to have survived in Central London. It had been surrounded by open countryside almost until the end of the 18th century; but as early as the 1840s the place was being engulfed by 'the tide of brick and mortar'. From that time onwards visitors began noting the abrupt transition between the urban world outside and the near miraculous oasis of rural peace that Lord Holland's estate had come to represent. Princess Liechtenstein, in her 1874 monograph on the Holland House, referred to 'those visitors who, tired with the rumble of carriages, or distracted by the crowd of fellow-creatures, rejoice in being able, even during the height of a London season, to transport themselves at a minute's notice into country calm and space.' Shortly afterwards a painting was exhibited at the Royal Academy that gave to Holland Park an idyllically rural aspect. Its title was *Five Miles from Charing Cross*.

For Londoners of today, so increasingly used to a mediocre world in which winter changes greyly and almost imperceptibly into spring and then into summer and autumn, Holland Park has the excitement of a place in which the passing of the seasons can be observed through the ever evolving spectacle of the trees and flowers. Snowdrops, daffodils, bluebells and crocuses grow among birches, cedars, limes and oaks, while elsewhere there are yuccas, magnolias, wisterias and a host of other exotic plants. This speckled, constantly changing backcloth ideally complements the motley human scenes to be witnessed in front of it. A remarkable cross-section of London society gathers daily in the park, from the young hooligans who wreak havoc on the flower beds to an astonishing array of the celebrities who live locally. The musician and media star Jarvis Cocker once remarked of this favourite haunt of his that, 'compared with Clapham Common, you get a much better class of oik loitering in the bushes.'

As your impressions of the park multiply, you will certainly become increasingly conscious of the place's single most famous feature – its peacocks. Though no-one seems to know quite when they were introduced here, they are a recurring motif in the many masterpieces of late 19th century decorative art to be found in the vicinity, such as Walter Crane's tiles at Leighton House, or the breath-taking 'Peacock' or Debenham House on Addison Road. The uncrowned rulers of the park, they seem to have responded to the repeated taunts of children by adopting an attitude of pure bloody-mindedness. The actor Derek Jacobi, while rehearsing for an adaptation of Dostoyevski's *The Idiot*, had little luck in trying to persuade them to do their high-pitched wail, which he had been told was like the cry of an epileptic. Generally, however, there is no stopping their crying, which adds – particularly during the mating season – a notoriously disruptive element to the classes given at the adjoining Holland Park School. In the case of the operas put on in the park between June and August, the sounds of these birds have become integral to the performances. 'Peacocks did duty for the tower's ravens', wrote the reviewer of a recent production of Gilbert and Sullivan's *Yeomen of the Guard*. Their contribution to the musical life of the park has even been honoured in a composition by the pianist Mary Leonard entitled *The Courtship of Two Peacocks in Holland Park.*

General view of Holland House from the south side, from Princess Liechtenstein's 1874 book on the house and its history

The wail of the peacock, so initially discordant and even absurd, comes eventually to seem like a haunting call beckoning you ever deeper into the park and its mysteries. You look more closely at the fragments from the past, and, as you do so, a story richer even than the place's natural attractions begins slowly to unravel.

The largest and oldest of these fragments is of course Holland House itself, which, in the late 19th century, was considered 'interesting to Londoners as the relic of an age and a phase of manners now long gone by.' The romantic associations that the house came to acquire are somewhat ironic in the light of the prosaic origins of the name 'Holland', which was a word used to describe a piece of low-lying land in need of drainage. Such a piece of land

was owned by one Sir Walter Cope, who, in 1604, began building on it what was originally a compact red brick block with decorative detailing derived from Flemish Renaissance art, and an overall late medieval look resulting largely from the massing of chimneys and ogee-caped turrets above the stepped and curved gables. Later, after the property had passed into the possession of Sir Walter's son-in-law Sir Henry Rich, the first Earl of Holland, wings and a projecting entrance were added to give the building the E-shaped plan characteristic of such great mansions of the period as Hatfield House. This new grandeur was furthered by the addition of a spectacular gate with elaborate piers designed by the greatest and most Italianate British architect of the day, Sir Inigo Jones. These piers still remain, albeit on a different site; but the house

itself, following Second World War bombing, London County Council demolitions, and drastic restoration, gives today only the palest idea of what it had once been like. Despite this, however, you can still appreciate what Princess Liechtenstein and others considered one of the house's most memorable attractions – the glimpses of brickwork to be had across lawns and through foliage. 'There is perhaps', wrote one 19th century commentator, 'no contrast in nature more pleasing than the artificial one between red brick and green trees'.

Though the present-days remains of Holland House do scant justice to the building's former greatness, there has survived in compensation a wealth of stories on which the imagination can feed. The first of these date from the time of Sir Henry Rich, a favourite of James I and Charles I who none the less was drawn to the personality and politics of Oliver Cromwell. Cromwell is said to have been a frequent visitor to Rich's estate, where he held meetings in open fields so as not to have his discussions overheard. Rich's divided allegiances were displayed in the Civil War, when he changed sides on a couple of occasions, and ended up suffering the same fate as Charles I, whose cause he had tokenly espoused at the end of the war. After his execution in 1649 he supplied Holland House with the first of the several ghost stories so apparently necessary to any English country mansion. With his severed head in his hands, he is supposed to appear at midnight from behind a secret door in the Gilt Room, which is above a dressing room now used by members of Holland Park's Opera Company.

Appropriately, the house's modern-day reputation for its opera performances was prefigured by the theatrical notoriety it gained under Sir Henry's distraught widow, who bravely put on plays here in defiance of the Puritans's ban on all such activities. The place's ghostly fame, meanwhile, was perpetuated by two of Sir Henry's grand-daughters, the Ladies Diana and Isabella. The former, according to the notorious gossip of the time, John Aubrey, was walking in the grounds of the house when 'she met with her own apparition, habit, and everything, as in a looking-glass. About a month after, she died. And it is said that her sister, the Lady Isabella, saw the like of herself also before she died. This account I had from a person of honour.' Thus a tradition was established that whenever the mistress of Holland House 'met herself', death would soon come to her. 'And so the old tradition has remained', wrote Princess Liechtenstein, 'and who would wish to remove it? Belonging to past times, it should be respected.'

As the ghosts accumulate so too do the memories of the famous people connected with Holland House. 'It is a great thing indeed', commented the author of an article on the house that appeared in *Country Life* in 1906, '...that the privileged can walk in the long avenues and by the fish-ponds of a former time. Almost at every step there is something to remind one of the great men who have visited the place – artists, architects, poets and statesmen.'

The first of the great literary figures associated with the place was the moralist, critic, satirist, and political commentator Joseph Addison, who in 1716 married the widowed daughter-in-law of the second Earl of Holland. The marriage was not a success, and a contemporary wit observed how Holland House, large as it was, 'could not contain Mr. Addison, the Countess of Warwick, and one guest, Peace.' Addison's love of drink seems to have increased during this time, and he supposedly regularly consumed a whole bottle of wine as he paced up and down the long gallery, absorbed in the composition of his works. Liver disease led probably to his death in the house in 1719. The writer George Tickell, in a poem commemorating his dead friend, conveyed the latter's love of strolling in the grounds of Holland House, which were evoked here for the first time with a sense of the transience of their beauty:

'How sweet were once thy prospects fresh and fair,
Thy sloping walks and unpolluted air.
How sweet the gloom beneath thy aged trees,
Thy noontide shadow, and thy evening breeze.'

The grounds known to Addison comprised fields, a number of formal plots around the house, a long straight walk directly south of the building, and – to the north – a 'wilderness' that was soon to be tamed by the creation of eight radiating avenues.

It was not until after 1746, when the house came to be occupied by Henry Fox, the first Lord Holland, that the park was developed in a more ambitious fashion. Fox called in a number of garden experts to advise him, including the celebrated landscape gardener William Kent, who designed the terraces near the house. But the most important contribution to the place was made by his close friend from Oxford days, the Hon. Charles Hamilton. Hamilton was responsible for numerous plantings, namely cedars, exotic American trees, and a 'vast variety of curious oaks'. His talents were fully displayed in the creation of the shady avenue known as the Green Walk, which now lies covered by Abbotsbury Road.

The Green Walk was a favourite haunt of Henry Fox's brilliant politician son Charles James Fox, who became a Whig MP when he was only nineteen. Though just his childhood was spent at

Holland House, memories of his early abode would affect him throughout his life. A touching account exists, by his biographer and contemporary Trotter, of what would be Fox's last visit to the house:

'He looked around him the last day he was there with a farewell tenderness that struck me very much. It was the place where he had spent his youthful days. Every lawn, garden, tree and walk, were viewed by him with particular affection. He pointed out its beauties to me, and in particular, shewed me a green lane or avenue...'

Already in Fox's day, under the occupancy of his nephew Henry, the third Lord Holland, Holland House was emerging as a brilliant centre of political and intellectual life. A bronze seated statue of the third Lord, designed by the painter

The Dutch Garden with a statue of Napoleon by Canova, from Princess Liechtenstein's 1874 book.

George Frederick Watt, and much favoured by pigeons, rises now above a pond on the northern, wooded side of the park. The podgy-faced man it portrays was a leading liberal politician with numerous intellectual passions, notably Napoleon and Spain. His interests were shared by his wife Elizabeth, a woman of forceful personality who was famous for her sharp tongue and unorthodox behaviour (the fact she had male servants make up her bed encouraged the painter Farrington to think of her as 'altogether a sensualist'). The dinners organized at their house were attended by luminaries from all over Europe, ranging from Spanish political exiles to Mme. de Stael and Sir Walter Scott. The historian Macaulay, an intimate member of the Holland circle, nostalgically recalled the house as 'the favourite resort of wits and beauties, of painters and poets, of scholars, philosophers and statesmen.' He remembered 'how the last debate was discussed in one corner, and the last comedy of Scribe in another; while Wilkie gazed with modest admiration on Reynolds's Baretti'; while Mackintosh turned over 'Thomas Aquinas' to verify a quotation; while Talleyrand related his conversations with Barras at the Luxembourg, or his ride with Lannes over the field at Austerlitz.'

Canova's bust of Napoleon, which was proudly displayed in the formal garden of Holland House after the emperor's exile to St. Helena (the Hollands's unpopular support of the Napoleonic cause was unflinching) was lost in the Second World War; but there are other vivid testimonies to this period. Not least of these is the formal garden itself, which was created in 1812 by the Italian factotum to the Holland family, Buonaiuti. Originally called the 'Portugese' Garden, the name was changed to 'Dutch Garden' after Britain's relations with

Portugal had deteriorated. The portion of this garden where Napoleon's bust could once be seen is now planted with dahlias, a flower that was first successfully introduced to England by Lady Holland herself, who brought it over from Spain.

Sheltered within a brick arbour directly across from the Dahlia Garden is a seat dedicated to Lord Holland's friend, Samuel Rogers, a banker poet who is best known today for having coined the phrase 'Not dead, but gone before'. An inscription above the bench, containing what Lord Holland referred to as 'some bad verses of mine in compliment to Rogers', records the poet's pleasure in sitting in this place where the Muse so often visited him. At one time you could also find here a poem by Rogers's contemporary Henry Luttrell, which reveals that inspiration did not come to everyone who sat within this bower:

'How lovely the scene! How propitious the hour!
The breeze is perfumed by the hawthorn it stirs;
All is beauty around me - but nothing occurs;
Not a thought, I protest-tho' I'm here and alone,
Not a line I can hit on that Rogers would own,
Though my senses are ravished, my feeling in tune,
And Holland's my host, and the season is June.'

Rogers' Seat, with Lord Holland's lines to his poet friend Samuel Rogers: 'Here Rogers sat, and here for ever dwell with me, those pleasures that he sings so well'

Those indulging in a sentimental tour of Holland Park are likely to become increasingly conscious of mortality as they continue tracing the history of the house and its gardens. The most dramatic death to have occured here was undoubtedly that of another friend of the third Lord Holland, Lord Camelford, to whom an antique Roman altar was afterwards erected, in the now empty ogee-arched aedicule further along the wall from 'Rogers's Seat'. This quarrelsome peer made the great mistake of challenging to a duel, on an outlying corner of the grounds, one of the best shots of his day, Captain Best. He fired first but missed, and then was shot through the body and lungs by his opponent. He died after two days in agony, nobly assuring all the time that he alone was to blame for what had happened.

The days of Holland House as a place of scintillating intellectual gatherings did not long survive the death of the third Lord Holland in 1840. His successor, Henry Edward Fox, who died without heir in 1859, spent long periods of his life away from London, mainly while serving as British Minister at the Court of Tuscany in Florence. His principal contribution to his

The conservatory with its original sculptural decoration

ancestral seat was the construction in 1849 of a garden Ball Room (now a restaurant run by Marco Pierre White), which continued to be the focus of lively and renowned garden parties right up to the 1930s. As a patron of the arts, the fouth Lord is best remembered for his support of George Frederick Watt, whom he met in Italy in 1843. Watt was put up in the Baron's Florentine Palace, and expected, wrongly, that he would subsequently be offered a permanent home at Holland House. Instead he was obliged to wheedle his way into becoming a lodger at a modest but delightful small property rented out by the Hollands to the artists Sara and Thoby Prinsep. This place, near the south end of Green Lane, was known officially as Little Holland House, but was referred to by its first owner as the 'Paradisino'.

Watt, in the words of his wife Mary, 'came to stay three days, and stayed thirty years'. His presence here was fundamental in turning the surroundings of Holland Park into a haven for successful artists.

'Little Holland House', sighed Mary Watt. 'Those three words evoke a picture of an enchanted garden, where it was always Sunday afternoon – afternoons prolonged, on rare red-letter days, into moonlit evenings full of music and delicate delights.' As with every paradise, however, the spectre of loss loomed in the background. In 1875 the house was demolished to make way for 'the insatiable maw of advancing London.' One of Watt's paintings of the park was of a grand cedar tree that had inspired from Rogers the lines, 'Majestic tree, whose wrinkled form has stood,/

Age after age, the patriarch of the wood'. Lord Wensleydale, in a parody of this, '...bet a thousand pounds – and time will show it, /That the stout tree survives the feeble poet.' However, he would have lost his money, for the tree died, together with almost all the fifty other cedars that had adorned the park in the early 19th-century. They were killed off by the fumes of London smoke.

On July 6, 1939, a grand dinner and ball were held at Holland House, attended by King George VI. This would be the last important social gathering held at the house, for, just over a year later, the place was gutted by fire as a result of an incendiary bomb. A telling photo exists of a group of men perusing the volumes in the burnt-out shell of the library. The park was left subsequently to decay, and soon was covered by weeds up to six

foot high; statuary and other ornaments were stored in the stableyard and garden ball-room, only to disappear completely. Further damage, according to the gardener's log book kept during the months immediately prior to the place's opening as a public park, was 'caused by the firing of three hundred rockets by the Royal Borough of Kensington (as a Coronation celebration)'.

No attempt was made to try and recreate the former splendour of Holland House, which was stripped of its most damaged parts, leaving intact only the east wing, which was drearily converted, by Sir Hugh Casson, into a youth hostel. But the grounds were gradually brought back to life, through restoration, replanting, the construction in 1962 of the imaginatively designed Commonwealth Institute, the holding of open-air art exhibitions,

An arcaded terrace above the Ball Room, today part of the Belvedere restaurant

The arcading leading to the Ball Room, as seen from what was once known as the Dutch Garden

the summer opera festival, and the creation in 1991 of a highly popular Japanese garden. Macaulay's vision of an expanding London that would one day 'displace those turrets and gardens, which are associated with so much that is interesting and noble', has fortunately proved wrong. And there are times – wandering, say, through central London's largest area of semi-natural woodland, or sitting contemplatively on Rogers's Seat, or attending an opera – when you can imagine yourself back to the magical domain evoked by so many writers and travellers of the past. The peacocks might be driving you mad; the children from the local comprehensive are momentarily distracting you; and rain (for this is England) is likely to be battering incessantly against the opera tent. Yet there remains something almost unworldly about Holland Park, as Gry Iverslien's photographs so beautifully convey.

Right. The North Gate, which was added when the public park was opened in 1952

Heralded by the appearance of the first snowdrops, spring soon transforms the park into a sweet-smelling, beautifully coloured carpet of daffodils, bluebells, magnolia, azalea and rhododendra.

Right The Green Lane that runs through the woodland on the northern end of the park is seen here with trees displaying their first leaves.

Above The fragrance of daffodils and other flowers enhances the spectacle of the spring.

Previous pages Lime Tree Walk with an avenue of daffodils.

Left The main gates at Kensington High Street were erected in 1836. Brought from Belgium by the third Lord Holland, they were flanked originally by two gatehouses that were later destroyed in the Second World War.

Above The east wing of Holland House seen from the south.

At the south side of the formal garden stands *Boy with Bear Cubs*, 1902, by John Macallan Swan (1847-1910). The sculpture has been on loan from the Tate Gallery since 1957. Holland House can be glimpsed in the background.

Above and right Along the woodland walk, bluebells carpet the undergrowth. Feeding cages and bird cages can be seen in the trees and on the ground.

Previous pages A peacock ascends the steps leading to the north lawn of Holland House.

Left This sculpture, *Tortoises with Triangle and Time*, by Wendy Taylor, is placed by the Abbotsbury Road entrance.

Above This ogee-arched aedicule or niche, incorporated into the wall of the formal gardens, might well have been intended to display a memorial to Lord Camelford, who was killed near here in 1804 while taking part in a duel.

Following pages The entrance to the formal garden from the north lawn is covered with wisteria. On the right is a 19th century Italian wall fountain.

Earth would be less fair without trees
to grace her valleys. Hide her scars
cast cool shade. In gardens here.

The Kyoto Garden is one of the most popular corners of the park. Designed and built by the Kyoto Garden Association in 1991, and officially opened by HRH The Prince of Wales and His Imperial Highness The Crown Prince of Japan, the place stands on the site of an early 19th century Japanese garden, one of the first of its kind in England.

Following pages Views of the Japanese Garden.

Previous pages and above Azalea Walk in late spring. From the north lawn is a path that leads to Holland Pond, where there is a statue (by G.F. Watts and J.E. Boehm) of the third Lord Holland, who turned his house into a celebrated meeting place for writers, intellectuals, and liberal politicians.

Above and right During the heyday of Holland House, at least twenty-seven gardeners were employed to look after its grounds. Today's gardeners, though far fewer in number, have the benefit of computers to control the climate of the three greenhouses reserved for bedding plants.

Right The quiet practice of Tai Chi is a regular sight in and around the park.

Following pages The Blue Indian peacock displaying its full plumage.

Left and above The Belvedere restaurant, run by Marco Pierre White, is situated in the former garden ballroom. Its cuisine and ambience give an added elegance to the park.

Following pages The sundial can be found at the far west side of the formal garden. Here it is seen touched by the early morning rays of the sun. In the background is a row of five arches comprising the remains of a nineteenth century stable block, which was connected to the former ballroom, now the Belvedere restaurant.

Summer reaches its height as the Dalhia Garden bursts into colour. Lady Holland imported this flower from Spain and was the first person successfully to grow them in England. Her husband, the third Lord Holland, thanked her in verse for doing so:

The dahlia you brought to our isle
Your praises forever shall speak
Mid gardens as sweet as your smile
And in colours as bright as your cheek.

Previous pages The south entrance of Holland House.

Above and right The east wing of Holland House, the main survival of the original Jacobean mansion, was converted in 1954 into the King George VI Memorial Youth Hostel.

Following pages A view from the woodland path of the north lawn.

Right In the stableyard are to be found booking and information offices, as well as an Ecology Centre featuring a permanent exhibition of the park's flora, fauna and wild life.

Previous pages Scenes of park life, including views of the sports field, the Commonwealth Institute, and the new adventure playground.

The northern woodlands form a small but important nature reserve. Over sixty species of birds have been seen in the park, amongst them, sparrowhawk, moorhen, woodpeckers, magpies, robins and herons. Squirrels, foxes and rabbits are also a common sight.

Right Moorhen chicks at the water edge.

Above Children catching tadpoles at the wildlife pond.

Left and above The east side view of the Orangerie and the Belvedere restaurant. The small terrace of the restaurant is a favourite place for lunch and dinner during the summer season.

Above and right The rose garden, in constant bloom throughout the summer, brings a dash of brilliant colour to the park.

Previous pages An interior view of the Orangerie featuring nineteenth century copies of two ancient bronzes of athletes, which were found in the Villa Papyri at Herculaneun. The Orangerie formed originally the conservatory of Holland House and was built in 1849 by the fourth Lord Holland. This light and elegant room is used today both as an art gallery and for social and commercial events.

Above left The south entrance to the Orangerie arcade.

Above right The park's cafe is partly situated under the tiled overhead walkway that runs in between the ice house and the ruins of Holland House.

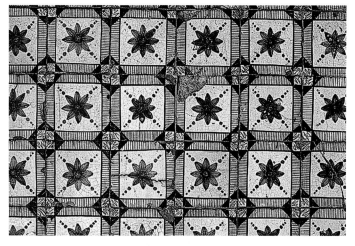

Twenty-three tiled panels of Italian origin line the
250-foot long overhead walkway, which was built
in 1849.

Above A selection of these tiles. See also image on
page 12.

Right The coats of arms of the Cope and Rich
families.

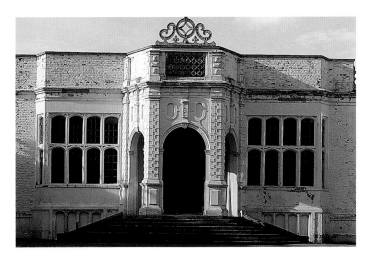

The Holland Park Theatre, the centre of outdoor opera in London, has for the last 30 years hosted musical events amongst the old ruins of Holland House. Today covered by a large canopy, performances take place over 10 weeks during June, July and August, with a select programme performed by the house company, Opera Holland Park and the Royal Philarmonic Orchestra.

Left and above Assembling the opera canopy. The ruins of the south front serve both as a dressing room and as a theatrical back-cloth that is in striking contrast to the temporary modern structure. The ghost of the first Earl of Holland, who is reputed to haunt the old building, has given this yearly event its own *Phantom of the Opera*.

Previous pages Holland House as seen from the formal garden during the opera season with the canopy extended over the ruins of the house.

Above One of the side porches at the south front of the House, here incorporating the opera terrace.

Right Opera lovers enjoying an area of Holland House that is normally closed to the public.

Previous pages A scene from the opera *Les Pecheurs de Perles* (Pearl Fishers) by Georges Bizet. (Costumes by Charles and Patricia Lester, set by Jamie Vartan).

Following pages (98-99) Flanking the Inigo Jones gateways are screens of terracotta medallions incorporating the Holland insignia.

Pages 100-101 The Orangerie Arcade, seen here on a summer evening, features a row of eleven paintings (by Mao Wen Biao) representing the celebrated garden parties held in the grounds of Holland House during the 1870s. In front of them stands a modern fountain by William Pye, which was installed in 1999. This part of the park is known as the Iris Garden.

With the arrival of autumn a soft bed of leaves covers the ground, and the park becomes a fiery composition of tawny reds and golds.

Above and left Two scenes from the Kyoto Garden.

Above Hidden away alongside the wall of the formal garden is an unidentified sculpture known as *The Ancient Melancholy Man.*

On a crisp, cold winter's morning nothing is more magical than seeing the lawns and old ruins of Holland Park sparkling with frost or covered under a blanket of virgin snow.

Above The frozen pond in the Kyoto Garden.

Right The stairs near the north gate.

Previous pages At the sloping lawn near the north gate, these sculptures (*Pyramids, Spheres* and *Cubes* by David Nash) were part of a sculpture exhibition celebrating the millennium.

Left The impressive gates to Holland House were
designed in 1629 by Inigo Jones and carved by
Nicholas Stone. They were earlier placed on the
north-east side of the house, but were moved to
their present position in 1959. The gate posts are
crowned with two griffins, holding respectively the
shields of the Rich and Cope families. Henry Rich
was the first Earl of Holland, who married Isabel,
daughter of Walter Cope, the builder of Holland
House.

Above left The Rich shield. *Above right* The Cope
shield.

Above This curious brick building, dating probably from the early nineteenth century, is a late example of an ice house, and was used originally for the storage of food which was kept in containers surrounded by straw. Today it serves as an art gallery.

Right The frozen Holland Pond with the sculpture *Journey* by Charlotte Mayer, on show during millennial sculpture exhibition.

Acknowledgements

For help in the production of this book we would like to thank The Royal Borough of Kensington and Chelsea, and in particular:

The Parks Service of the Environment and Leisure Business Group.

The Local History section in Kensington Central Library for the information sources for the text and for permission to use images. Our thanks to the Library Manager, Amber Baylis.

The Friends of Holland Park and Rhoddy Wood for permission to use one photograph (pp.126-127) by the late Christopher Wood, whose booklet *H Is For Holland* has been an enormous help to us both.

Carolyn Starren for her good advice.

Lastly, a very special thanks to John McEachen, Head of Libraries and Arts, for his encouragement and enthusiasm during the production of this work.

The interior photograph on page 61 is published courtesy of The Belvedere Restaurant.